# Figures for an Apocalypse

Publishing Genius Press
www.PublishingGenius.com

ISBN 13: 978-0-9887503-4-0

Cover design by the author
Page design by Adam Robinson

First Edition
October 2013
Copyright © Edward Mullany 2013

# BOOK I

| | |
|---|---|
| 5 | The Doppelgängers |
| 6 | The Man Who Beat His Dog |
| 7 | The Birthmarks |
| 8 | The Television Incident |
| 9 | The Wrong Child |
| 11 | The Levitation of the Fast Food Restaurant |
| 12 | The Mannequin's Tears |
| 13 | Curtains |
| 15 | A Minnesota Divorce |
| 16 | The Sitcom |
| 17 | The Cows That Were Eaten By Other Cows |
| 18 | The Silent City |
| 19 | The Man in the White Suit |
| 20 | The Comatose Woman |
| 21 | The Suffering Channel |
| 22 | The Propaganda |
| 23 | The Information |
| 25 | The Return of the Guillotine |
| 26 | The Voice From the Sky |
| 27 | The White Labyrinth |
| 28 | Only Wall |
| 29 | The Teething |
| 30 | The Insane Laughter |
| 31 | Contagion |
| 33 | The Burned Photographs |
| 34 | The Water That Tasted Like Blood |
| 35 | The Lamentations |
| 36 | The Suicide Note |
| 37 | The Coroner's Report |
| 38 | The Riddle |

| | |
|---|---|
| 39 | The Police |
| 40 | Reunion |
| 42 | The Plague |
| 43 | The Swarm of Mosquitoes |
| 44 | The House That Fell Into the Sea |
| 45 | The Man in the Coffin |
| 46 | The Suspect |
| 47 | The Man Without a Face |
| 48 | The Dead Dog |
| 49 | The Defendant |
| 50 | The Warden |
| 51 | The Warden's Wife |
| 52 | The Verdict |
| 53 | The Side Effects |
| 54 | The Empty Airport |
| 55 | A Story Without an Ending |
| 56 | The Black Holes |
| 57 | The Wooden Boy |
| 58 | The Sinner's House |
| 59 | The Ammunition |
| 60 | The Cities That Remained |
| 61 | The Televisions |
| 62 | The Boiling of the Liars |
| 63 | The Three Dogs |
| 64 | A Comedy for the Old West |

# Figures for an Apocalypse

EDWARD MULLANY

Publishing Genius
Baltimore

# Book II

| | |
|---|---|
| 69 | The Cup of Tears |
| 70 | Bushfire |
| 71 | The Children Who Ran Rampant |
| 72 | The Internet Baby |
| 73 | The Girl Whose Eyes Were Sewn Shut |
| 74 | The Room Full of Amputated Limbs |
| 75 | Sims |
| 76 | The Churches That Burned |
| 77 | The Sea |
| 78 | The Statues of Weeping Women |
| 79 | The Birds That Hadn't Perished |
| 80 | The Disappearance of Shopping Malls |
| 81 | The Men Who Jumped to Their Deaths |
| 82 | The Argument About Which Typeface to Use |
| 83 | A Rugged Coast |
| 84 | The Golden Palace |
| 85 | The Boy Who Was Drawn and Quartered |
| 86 | The Flogging |
| 87 | The Perpetual Light |
| 88 | The Enormous Spiders |
| 89 | Dookie |
| 90 | The Ghosts of Men Who Died Without Confessing Their Sins |
| 91 | The Love Factory |
| 92 | Say No |
| 93 | The Father Who Drove His Family Over a Cliff |
| 94 | The House Full of Clocks |
| 95 | The Mothers Who Refused to Kill Their Children |
| 96 | The Domestication of Frogs |
| 97 | The Day Painkillers Fell From the Sky |

| | |
|---|---|
| 98 | The Forbidden Melody |
| 99 | The Woman Without a Face |
| 100 | The Balaclavas |
| 101 | The Last Film |
| 102 | The Battleaxes |
| 103 | The Fish |
| 104 | Seconds |
| 105 | The Drawing of the Three |
| 106 | The Forgotten Story |
| 107 | The Man with the Straight Blade |
| 108 | The Knives That Were Found on the Highways |
| 109 | The Banning of Music |
| 110 | The Soldier Who Cried |
| 111 | The Absolution |
| 112 | Randolph |
| 113 | The New Crucifixions |
| 114 | The Hope |
| 115 | The Zoo Without Creatures |

# Book III

| | |
|---|---|
| 121 | The Mirrored Hall |
| 122 | The Names of the Dead |
| 123 | The Witch |
| 124 | The Bloodletting |
| 125 | Desperado |
| 126 | The Famine |
| 127 | The Envy |
| 128 | The Men on the Beach |
| 129 | The Workaholic |
| 130 | The Sadness of Trees |
| 131 | The Avalanche |
| 132 | Mike, Thirteen |
| 133 | The Offspring |
| 134 | The Paranoid Cat |
| 135 | The Stairs That Went Nowhere |
| 136 | The Ecstatic Vision |
| 137 | The Assassin |
| 138 | The Defenestration |
| 139 | The Absence of Friends |
| 140 | The House in the Country |
| 141 | The House Full of Human Hair |
| 142 | The Machine Gun Song |
| 143 | The Parade of Rabbits |
| 144 | The Man Found Guilty of Contempt |
| 145 | The Good Pagan |
| 146 | The Killers |
| 147 | Honeymoon |
| 148 | The Man Who Refrained From Speaking |
| 149 | The Joy That Was Mistaken for Sorrow |
| 150 | The Battle That Was Lost Before it Was Begun |

| | |
|---|---|
| 151 | The Tin Drum |
| 152 | The Snow |
| 153 | The Holy Water |
| 154 | The Sky Beneath the Sky |
| 155 | Single |
| 156 | The Book That Wouldn't Burn |
| 157 | The Annulment |
| 158 | The Winding Sheet |
| 159 | The Women Who Spoke in Quiet Voices |
| 160 | The River |
| 161 | The Drums of Heaven |
| 162 | The Good Thief |
| 163 | Forty-three |
| 164 | The Woman Who Lived in the Desert |
| 165 | The Narrow Road to the Interior |
| 166 | The Other Laura |
| 167 | Dead |
| 168 | The Two Horses |
| 169 | The Trance |
| 170 | The Warrant |
| 171 | A Working Lunch |
| 172 | The Fastest Gun in the West |
| 173 | The Three Spies |
| 174 | The Man Who Collected Teeth |
| 175 | The Lover |
| 176 | The Hunter and the Hound |
| 177 | The Apostle |
| 178 | The Tree and the Sky |
| 179 | New Year |
| 180 | The Sea of Galilee |
| | |
| 183 | Acknowledgements |

# BOOK I

And in those days men shall seek death, and shall in no wise find it; and they shall desire to die, and death fleeth from them.

*Revelation 9:6*

# THE DOPPELGÄNGERS

One morning, talking on a phone as he wandered with his dog on a beach, a man passed a man who was talking on a phone as he wandered with his dog on the beach.

# THE MAN WHO BEAT HIS DOG

He worked near the top floor of one of the city's many office buildings, which meant that every weekday morning, or *most* weekday mornings—for some days were holidays, or days he called in sick—he was obliged to move vertically through space to a height at which humans didn't ordinarily exist. He could take the elevator or the stairs, though to take the stairs he would have to exert himself to an unusual degree, and would have to allow the people with whom he worked, and who'd realized he'd taken the stairs, to regard him with amused disbelief.

# THE BIRTHMARKS

One day, every child

born was born
with the same one.

# THE TELEVISION INCIDENT

A man was sitting on a couch with a remote control when the remote control

bit him.

# THE WRONG CHILD

She ate lunch, with some of her classmates, at one of the long, wheeled folding tables that were set up by the janitor in the gymnasium during the lunch hour. Then she went out to the playground with some of her classmates and stood in a huddled group, talking with them, or listening to them talk (and sometimes laughing or joining in with their laughter), while around them other classmates ran wildly. After recess, when a teacher appeared near a door near the entrance to the building, with one arm raised, as an indicator that recess was over, she crossed the playground quickly and went inside with all her classmates, and went up a stairwell, and down a hall, and into the classroom she always went into that year, and sat in the desk she'd begun to think of as her own. After a few more hours, during which her teacher spoke in a droning, unenthusiastic voice, and she wrote with a pencil in a notebook she was accustomed to writing in—sometimes looking out the window—she heard a voice come over the intercom, announcing end-of-day activities, and requesting certain students who'd misbehaved that day to appear in the principal's office. Into her bookbag, which hung from a hook in the hall outside the classroom, she put the books she knew she'd need at home to do her homework. Then she went outside with one of her friends, walking slowly, and talking about something that had happened that day, or about something that might happen tomorrow. A car driven by her mother was waiting for her in the street. The sky was bright; it hadn't rained. "See you," she said to her friend, who, smiling, said, "see you" in return. Then she got into the car, and went or was taken home.

# THE LEVITATION OF THE FAST FOOD RESTAURANT

There was the sound of concrete breaking as the building lifted,

or was lifted,

from its foundation.

# THE MANNEQUIN'S TEARS

The editor of the newspaper in the town that was home to the department store where they had first been sighted said to a reporter, "Well, we may as well do a story on it. Go on down there, and take a photographer with you."

# CURTAINS

Dabovitch got fired.

He told his wife that evening.

First she was standing and he was sitting. Then he was standing and she was standing. Then she was sitting and he was pacing. Then she was standing at the sliding door that looked out of their apartment into the lot. It was after sunset.

"I was going to quit anyway," Dabovitch said from somewhere behind her. His tie was loosened and he had the short, close-cropped beard of a middle manager.

"Going to," said his wife, as if speculations were irrelevant. In her mind they *were* irrelevant, though sometimes her definition of speculation varied.

Dabovitch went into the kitchen for a beer.

But he didn't get one.

He was afraid now how it would look to his wife. He was also afraid how it would look if he didn't get one, so he removed a can from the fridge and set it on the counter.

But this was no good either.

His wife entered the kitchen and leaned against the doorjamb. She was a very pretty woman with tired eyes. She worked too. They would never be rich. They were just old enough now to realize it. "Look at you," she said.

"What," said Dabovitch, though not because he hadn't heard her. He was in love with her more than she was in love with him.

"What would happen," said his wife, "if I told you now I was pregnant?"

His eyes went wide. He moved toward her, but stopped when she laughed.

An hour passed.

Neither of them made dinner.

When it was dark they were both sitting on the couch.

# A MINNESOTA DIVORCE

"A favor it is *not*," Lena said to her husband, or to the man who was still technically her husband. They were standing in their kitchen at sundown on a winter afternoon. The cat was looking in from the window ledge, hoping or expecting that someone would let it in. It had no expression on its face.

"If it results in us all being happier," said her husband, and then, because she tried to interrupt him, he said it again, in a louder, more articulate voice, though without finishing the sentence.

A boy and a girl came home. The cat ran into the kitchen ahead of them, shook the cold from itself, and stood for a moment on the center of the linoleum while the children were stamping their boots.

# THE SITCOM

In a white
field, a man and two

women walked. "Is there
a God?" asked the man.

"No," said the first woman.
"No," said the second woman.

## THE COWS THAT WERE EATEN BY OTHER COWS

were there years
later, their white

bones stringy
with flesh.

# THE SILENT CITY

On the sidewalks and in the streets

lay the birds that had suddenly fallen.

# THE MAN IN THE WHITE SUIT

He grinned
and grinned
and grinned
and grinned
and grinned.

# THE COMATOSE WOMAN

She was in a car accident in which both the driver of the car in which she had been riding and the driver of the car in which she had not been riding had been found to not be at fault.

# THE SUFFERING CHANNEL

People had to prepare themselves to watch it; that is, they had to make certain ablutions. A man would quickly shave his face, and comb his hair with water, while a woman would wear a fresh dress made of white linen. No child made ablutions because no child was allowed to watch it.

# THE PROPAGANDA

It was written in excellent

penmanship.

# THE INFORMATION

There was a baseball diamond at the end of his street. He went there with his kids. Two of his kids were girls, so they just ran around in the outfield, or pulled up daisies, not that he expected them to be disinterested in baseball. But he wanted them to take an interest in what *they* wanted to take an interest in. Would people understand this? Seeing him hitting grounders to his son, who was indisputably unskilled, but who, more than anyone he had encountered, was enthusiastic about the game, would they wonder why the girls could not be involved? That the girls themselves had declined their father's invitation to play, people might not be aware of. They would look upon the scene with the ignorance, or naivety, of bystanders. They would assume the way bystanders would assume, perhaps not with malice—because, after all, what was a little baseball?—but certainly with the degree of condescension that comes from not knowing all the relevant information.

For instance, how could they be sure, now that it was mid-afternoon and the sun had been out all day, that *he* was sure the girls didn't need more sunscreen? Of course, this wouldn't be the first thought that entered their minds. They themselves were out in the sun. They were walking in the very same park, under the very same sky. Conversation that would be continuing from an earlier stage in their walk wouldn't come to a halt, or, if it did, its mood wouldn't simply disintegrate, allowing them to discuss the scene before their eyes with cool, scientific detachment. They would have to make transitions, emotional as well as logical. They would have to say—think, rather, because he didn't want to put words in their mouths—"Now here is this man playing baseball with his son and not with his daughters. Is this okay?"

# THE RETURN OF THE GUILLOTINE

"Absolutely," said the first man.
"Absolutely," said the second man.

"Maybe," said the third man.

But then he changed his mind and said, "Absolutely, absolutely."

# THE VOICE FROM THE SKY

Go or don't go. Stay
or don't stay. I have seen

this day before this day
arrived.

# THE WHITE LABYRINTH

Out of it walked a naked
man and two

naked women.

# ONLY WALL

Tired, I get out of bed in the morning. I brush my teeth. But then I get back in bed, and accidentally fall asleep for another hour. "Where are you?" my boss asks when he calls. "On the train," I say. "It was delayed." "How can you be on the train?" he says. "There's no reception on the train." The truth is I'm still in bed. He woke me when he called. I get out of bed, brush my teeth again hurriedly, and soon am really on the train, which is less full than it is at my usual hour. "I brushed my teeth twice this morning," I say to an old woman next to me, and I grin at her as if I'm a little crazy. "Whatever for?" she says. Then she says, "You young people are all the same," and she gets up and moves to the other end of the carriage. The train slows as it enters the station at which I usually get off. But it doesn't completely stop. I look out the windows and see the faces of other commuters as the train passes the spots on the platform at which they've chosen to stand. Then the train is in the tunnel again, and out the windows I can see only wall.

# THE TEETHING

When the woman heard the baby start crying in the middle of the night, she lay still for a moment, wondering whether her husband had woken, and, if he *had* woken, whether he would get up and go out to the other room, where the baby's crib was, and try to quiet the baby while she herself fell back to sleep, or while she stayed awake, listening to him try to quiet the baby.

# THE INSANE LAUGHTER

There were two queues: one you waited in,

and one you waited in
to get into the one you waited in.

# CONTAGION

Tammy's mother had the flu, but when she tried to call work, the line was busy. "I'll take Tammy to school," said Tammy's father. "You keep trying work till I get back, then I'll take over for you." "What if you get the flu too?" said Tammy's mother. "This phone's probably covered in germs by now. No, you take Tammy to school, as you said, but when you get back I'll keep calling work myself, unless I've already gotten through, in which case all you'll need to do is let me sleep." "Agreed," said Tammy's father.

But on the way to school, he realized he was coming down with the flu too. "I can't kiss you goodbye," he said to Tammy. "I can blow you a kiss like this, but I can't get any closer." He blew her a kiss, and Tammy started crying. She wouldn't say what she was crying about, but Tammy's father understood it could have been any number of things. "Okay," he said, "okay," and he got out of the car and helped her on with her backpack. Other mothers were there, chatting in twos and threes, and some of them were giving him curious looks, as if they weren't sure he belonged. "I'm going to stand right here," he said. "You go on and find your friends, and when you find them you wave to me so I know everything is all right. If you don't find them, or if you find them but you don't feel like they are welcoming you, you come right on back to me and we'll figure out something else." "But I want you to come inside with me," Tammy said. "I want you to see what my classroom is like. You've never seen what my classroom is like because you've never been in my classroom."

Tammy's father crouched down so his eyes were level with Tammy's. He was going to explain to her the nature of the contagion, how it could spread easily from person to person, especially in a school, where so many kids came in close physical contact with each other, and how his visiting the classroom might do more harm than good. But just then a mother came up to them and put a hand on Tammy's shoulder. "Hi sweetie," she said. "I'm Carol Ann's mother, you remember Carol Ann don't you?" She was saying all this while looking at Tammy, but somehow Tammy's father felt it was for his benefit. "Hi," he said cheerfully, though he didn't extend his hand. "Tammy here wants her father to see her classroom, but Tammy's father doesn't want to give either her or Carol Ann, or any of their other friends, any of his nasty germs." "Well I think that's a very noble gesture," said Carol Ann's mother, who now had been joined by Carol Ann herself, a little girl the same height as Tammy. The two little girls joined hands, and spoke to each other in sweet, quiet voices.

"I also have the flu," said Carol Ann's mother, "or at least I'm in the early stages of it. How is Tammy's mother feeling? She must not be feeling well if you've had to come in her stead, not that I'm sorry you did." Tammy's father glanced at Carol Ann's mother and saw what he was looking for, though if he'd had to describe what it was he'd been looking for he would have been unable to. Standing to his full height, he reached out and tousled Tammy's hair, which he'd never done before, and which caused Tammy to look at him strangely. "Go on, you two," said Carol Ann's mother, and she had to say it again, this time in a lighter voice, and with an almost artificial enthusiasm, as if persuading the little girls, before the two of them went away. But even after they went away they kept looking back.

# THE BURNED PHOTOGRAPHS

They were piled

in the corner of a room that had no
ceiling.

# THE WATER THAT TASTED LIKE BLOOD

It came out of the faucet of a kitchen sink into a cup no one was holding.

# THE LAMENTATIONS

On the side of a mountain, above the tree line, but below the altitude at which snow could remain without melting, smoke curled from the chimney of a wood cabin. Inside the cabin, a man slept. Outside, across the ground, the shadows of clouds moved.

# THE SUICIDE NOTE

He wrote it and then
crumpled it and then

put it in his mouth.

# THE CORONER'S REPORT

I am an old man now.

Or I am a young man
who describes himself as old.

# THE RIDDLE

"Whisper it in my ear," a woman at a cocktail party told a man who wasn't the man with whom she'd arrived. The man leaned toward her, grinning, but when his lips got near enough to her that, if he whispered, the woman would be able to hear him, the man with whom the woman had arrived saw what was happening, and said, "That's enough, get away from her, she came to this party with me."

# THE POLICE

There was a telephone on a table in a hall.

It started ringing.
"Can you get that?" a woman called.

# REUNION

Jack and I were at the department store, and, as usual, Jack didn't want to be there, only this time he'd come with someone else.

I sat with him on the edge of one of those nice-looking beds. I'd been shopping all day, so in a way I was able to rationalize it.

From a nearby fitting room came the voice of a woman who evidently believed Jack was the only one who could hear her. We looked at each other with raised eyebrows. I knew who the woman was. But Jack and I had been divorced long enough to know that speaking of each other's mates when those mates weren't there to defend themselves inevitably led to suspicions of jealously, even if what was said was meant to be funny, so we'd made it a rule to keep our mouths shut.

"You'd better go see what she wants," I said, and lifted one of my shopping bags in her direction.

Jack got up, but not before looking inside the bag. It was Christmas, and old habits die hard.

"What's going on?" said the woman from the fitting room. She'd come out in a nightgown that looked better on her than it would have on me, but when she'd seen us she'd stopped, as if the sight of us together had made her forget why she was here.

"It's all right," said Jack. "You look great, sweetheart. Is that the one you want?"

The woman looked at me. Jack's hand was still in my shopping bag. He took it out slowly, like a child caught in the act of something insidious. I didn't say anything. But I did something I knew would communicate what I wanted to tell her, something that, even though I despised myself for it, I found myself unable to help. I smiled in a way that was suggestive rather than friendly, and arched just one of my eyebrows. The woman turned away in tears.

Later, when I met my husband in the mall, he tried to peek inside the shopping bag like Jack had done, but it wasn't the same, and I snapped at him.

# THE PLAGUE

Somewhere, a man played the violin

while standing naked in a hotel room

he had emptied of everything not

bolted to the floor.

# THE SWARM OF MOSQUITOES

It moved toward the city.
Then it moved through the city.
Then it continued on out

the other side of the city.

# THE HOUSE THAT FELL INTO THE SEA

In it lived a family

who were like other families who
thought they were not

like other families.

# THE MAN IN THE COFFIN

His face was white.
His suit was black.
His lips were red.

# THE SUSPECT

She left the motel before dawn, dropping a suitcase in the trunk of a vehicle she was about to get into.

# THE MAN WITHOUT A FACE

People took his photograph, or turned quickly

or slowly

away.

# THE DEAD DOG

A girl walked

down the street,

carrying it.

# THE DEFENDANT

When asked by the judge whether he had anything he'd like to say in his own defense, he said, "Yes."

"Well," said the judge, "Go ahead."

"Go ahead what?" he said.

"Say what you'd like to say in your defense," said the judge.

"I already said it," he said.

"What—'*Yes?*'" said the judge, surprised and a little annoyed.

"Yes," he said again.

# THE WARDEN

One night, after his wife had woken him because she'd had a bad dream and was afraid of what it might mean, he couldn't fall back to sleep, even after she herself had fallen back to sleep.

# THE WARDEN'S WIFE

When he was at work,

she prayed or thought

about praying.

# THE VERDICT

Outside, the sun

shone on every

blade of grass.

# THE SIDE EFFECTS

First he lost his hair.
Then he began to shrink.
Then his skin turned a weird

pink. Then he died.

# THE EMPTY AIRPORT

A woman holding the hand of a little girl stood for a long time, staring and not saying anything, before turning and beginning to walk quickly, and then run, in the direction of the doors through which she and the little girl had entered.

# A STORY WITHOUT AN ENDING

I'd been stabbed by a man wielding a six-inch kitchen knife on a train moving very fast through part of the tunnels that had been built underneath the city, but now the man was gone, and two strangers, neither of whom knew each other, but both of whom had been the only other passengers in this carriage, had come to my aid, and the train itself was slowing as it entered the next station. "Breathe slowly," said one of the strangers, a man, because my breathing had gotten fast and irregular, but also, perhaps, because he didn't know what else to say to me. The other stranger, a woman, didn't say anything, but she pressed her hand over my hand, which itself was pressing against the wound in my chest, and she kept watching the door at the end of the carriage through which the man with the knife had hurried.

# THE BLACK HOLES

How and why did
not matter as much

as when and where and how
many.

# THE WOODEN BOY

"I am the wooden boy," said the wooden
boy to the wooden
girl.

# THE SINNER'S HOUSE

You came upon it in the forest, having wandered for many days and nights, lost. You said to yourself, "I'm going to knock," and then you knocked.

# THE AMMUNITION

Among the men was a man who worried aloud that they, as a group, wouldn't have enough. "What if we run out?" he said. The others looked at him, and then at each other, not having thought of this, or having thought of this but not having said it.

# THE CITIES THAT REMAINED

There were crimes, but no sirens.

## THE TELEVISIONS

Some were on and some
were off. Some had been spattered

with goat's
blood.

# THE BOILING OF THE LIARS

First, it was dark. Then the sun began to come up. Then a crowd began to gather. Then a group of naked men and women were led out into the courtyard.

# THE THREE DOGS

The first one died.
It lay down in the street, and couldn't or wouldn't get up.
The second one and the third one waited near it for some time.
They whined a little, sniffing the cold air.

# A COMEDY FOR THE OLD WEST

The sheriff said he had too many deputies, that one of them had to go. "Not me," said Southpaw. "Me neither," said Sticks. "Then you'll have to flip for it," said the sheriff. "Do either of you have a coin?" Both men fished in their trouser pockets, but came up empty-handed. "Mary-Beth?" said the sheriff, calling to the secretary in the next room. A little gray-haired woman came in. "Do you have a coin?" the sheriff asked. "No, sheriff, I sure don't," said Mary-Beth. "Want me to go make change next door?" "Yes, Mary-Beth, why don't you do that. Meanwhile, Southpaw and Sticks and I'll wait here till you get back." Mary-Beth went out. The sheriff sat himself in the chair behind his desk, raised his boots, crossed them on the desk. Southpaw and Sticks looked at each other. The afternoon sun came through the window and shone on the wood floor.

# BOOK II

I know of thy doings, and see,
I have set before thee an open door, there is no shutting it.

*Revelation 3:8*

# THE CUP OF TEARS

"I'll tell you a story," the mother said to the little boy, who'd asked to hear a story. "Once there was a road that led to a city that wasn't burned."

# BUSHFIRE

There is a song that is whispered, there is an inhuman voice.

There is a skeleton that walks across the desert.

# THE CHILDREN WHO RAN RAMPANT

You could hear them at night,
while you tried to sleep,
or while you tried to stay

awake so that if they found
you they wouldn't find you
asleep.

# THE INTERNET BABY

It wasn't that it cried
but that it cried

and laughed simultaneously.

# THE GIRL WHOSE EYES WERE SEWN SHUT

There was a chair in the center of a round room. On this she sat.

# THE ROOM FULL OF AMPUTATED LIMBS

It had no door.
Or it had a door that was always locked.
Or it had a door that was always unlocked but that no one was willing to open.

# SIMS

Sims gets home late. His home is in the good neighborhood on the hill.

"Hello?" he says, putting his briefcase down in the kitchen.

He goes upstairs.

He glances in the master bedroom, though he knows it is unlikely anyone will be in there yet. His wife is in there, sleeping, or pretending to sleep. She's not under the covers, but is lying on her side, in all her clothes, facing away from him.

# THE CHURCHES THAT BURNED

You could go in them and sit by yourself in a blackened pew, and look up at the sky through the space where the roof had once been. Maybe someone else would be in there too—an old woman hiding her face behind a shawl, or a young man curious or bored. Sometimes a rafter that had been damaged but had not yet fallen would fall.

# THE SEA

It was orange, one
week, pink

the next.

# THE STATUES OF WEEPING WOMEN

Along empty highways they

were placed at equal

intervals.

# THE BIRDS THAT HADN'T PERISHED

Didn't they recognize the change
the world had undergone? They sang

in the morning, roosted
at night. They bit fingers

off the corpses of men.

# THE DISAPPEARANCE OF SHOPPING MALLS

There is a kind of music
that has not yet been written

or that has been written but has not yet
been heard.

# THE MEN WHO JUMPED TO THEIR DEATHS

One night they met at the top of a cliff that looked out over a sea that had long been absent of boats or ships or other sea-worthy vessels. They knelt together, and moved their lips in silence, each reciting the same prayer, before getting up and standing in a long line along the edge of the cliff.

# THE ARGUMENT ABOUT WHICH TYPEFACE TO USE

Men in suits and women in power suits sat around a huge polished conference table in a building so high you couldn't see the top.

# A RUGGED COAST

"Why do you hate nature?" asked the boy's stepmother, who didn't actually believe the boy hated nature, but believed he wanted her to believe he hated nature.

"He doesn't hate nature," said his father.

They were looking out at the sea, a wind was blowing in their faces, and it was cold.

"How do you know what I hate?" said the boy.

"He knows what you hate because he's your father," said his stepmother lightheartedly.

"No," said his father. "I know what he hates because he's my son."

# THE GOLDEN PALACE

It was rumored to be somewhere
in a desert in the country that had once

been known as America.

# THE BOY WHO WAS DRAWN AND QUARTERED

There are two photographs
of him: one in the moment

his sentence is carried out,
and one in the moment before

the moment his sentence
is carried out.

# THE FLOGGING

You could pay
to watch. The

more you could
pay, the closer

you would be
seated.

# THE PERPETUAL LIGHT

It happened like this: one day the sun

did not set.

# THE ENORMOUS SPIDERS

They were big enough to eat bears though
they did not eat bears they
ate men.

# DOOKIE

A man in a suit and tie walks out of his house one morning, gets in his car, which has been parked in his and his wife's driveway overnight, and backs the car into the street, where it hits, or is hit by, another car—this one driven by a man who minutes earlier had backed out of his own driveway, less than a mile away, and had driven at a not unusual speed through the circuitous streets of the suburb in which he and the other man live. Both men get out and survey the damage to their vehicles. The engines of their cars now are off. Their mouths are closed tight, like fists. The wife of the man who has just left the house has opened the front door, and is looking cautiously out, wearing a bathrobe. A little girl whose head reaches the woman's waist is trying to poke her head around to see.

# THE GHOSTS OF MEN WHO DIED WITHOUT CONFESSING THEIR SINS

You couldn't see

them but you

could hear them and they

could touch you.

# THE LOVE FACTORY

You didn't just meet someone. Every Saturday morning, in certain towns in certain areas of certain states, the doors to a large gray building were opened, and a certain number of citizens who'd lined up the night before were allowed in, two by two.

# SAY NO

My mother decided to remarry.

But at the last minute she and the guy got in an argument.

I went to his house and punched him one in the face.

It was a big house. Behind him, in the long dimly-lit hall, I could see people milling around, laughing and conversing and so forth.

"You're having a party?" I said.

To show his magnanimity, or perhaps because he simply was magnanimous, he let me in. But nobody wanted to speak to me. They'd all seen what I'd done. They looked upon me as if I was part of the lower class, which I was. I went back out and sat on the stoop. He followed me out with an icepack on his nose.

Neither of us spoke.

There were things I wanted to say, but the more I thought about them, the less important they seemed.

Finally my mother showed up.

She didn't know I'd come here.

I hid in the bushes so that when she got to the stoop she'd say what was on her mind.

# THE FATHER WHO DROVE HIS FAMILY OVER A CLIFF

He had a red beard.
He had red eyes.
He worked in a red office.
He drank red milk.

# THE HOUSE FULL OF CLOCKS

You could open the door, but you could not go in. There was no room.

# THE MOTHERS WHO REFUSED TO KILL THEIR CHILDREN

They were studied by clinicians who wore white lab coats and who jotted notes on clipboards in a large, brick building that was located out in the country. This was after they had been taken from their homes one night while they slept or tried to sleep, and had been blindfolded, loaded into the back of armored lorries, and driven out to the large brick building that housed the clinicians who would study them.

# THE DOMESTICATION OF FROGS

One morning, a man in a boardroom way high up above the streets of what had once been a city, announced to other men in the boardroom that the time had come for the domestication of frogs. At first, the other men in the boardroom were hesitant to agree, and murmured their hesitations, but the man whose idea it had been showed them pie charts and bar graphs, and recited various statistics, and eventually he prevailed upon them.

# THE DAY PAINKILLERS FELL FROM THE SKY

The weather was clear.

# THE FORBIDDEN MELODY

Some of the older

folks still knew it.

# THE WOMAN WITHOUT A FACE

Two men walked
down an alley

at night, passing
a bottle back

and forth. "Did
you hear that?" one

said, suddenly
stopping. "Hear

what?" said the
other, unsure

whether to laugh
or be afraid.

# THE BALACLAVAS

They were to be worn
at all times, by women

and by men, not only
when it was cold, but

when it was hot.

# THE LAST FILM

It was screened in a cinema that seated nine million people.

# THE BATTLEAXES

The important thing was to find one you could wield with the most efficiency. This did not necessarily mean finding the lightest, but rather the one whose blade was just heavy enough to cause a deathblow each time you swung it.

# THE FISH

First there was one song.
Then there were two songs.
Then there were two

songs and a glass of whiskey.

# SECONDS

Finally the woman whose head had been picked up by the man who'd beheaded her died.

# THE DRAWING OF THE THREE

A boy with no mouth lives
in a house with no windows.

Two women wearing red
lipstick fight in a mall, or

three women wearing red
lipstick walk arm in arm

into an ocean they will not
come out of.

# THE FORGOTTEN STORY

In a desert, a man with a long beard told another man with a long beard that he believed they would soon find water. "When is soon?" asked the second man. "Today? Tomorrow? Don't tell me 'soon'. Neither of us has any idea if or when we'll find water. We're both lost." They did not find water. The first man died, and, a little while later, the second man died.

# THE MAN WITH THE STRAIGHT BLADE

He was standing in the shadows on my porch one night, waiting for me, or for someone he thought was me, as I returned from work. My family was inside. The light in the living room was burning. I could see them laughing at something they were watching on TV.

# THE KNIVES THAT WERE FOUND ON THE HIGHWAYS

The number of trucks required
to remove them

was higher than the number
of trucks that existed.

# THE BANNING OF MUSIC

Against the trunk of a tree in a field out in the country sat a man and a woman who'd removed their clothes many seasons ago and who now were dead.

# THE SOLDIER WHO CRIED

He began one night in the barracks, while his comrades slept, and he continued all night and on into the next morning and well on into the afternoon.

# THE ABSOLUTION

There was a TV channel that never went off the air. What it broadcast was this: a man wearing a suit and tie seated behind a desk. Behind him was a white screen. The man smiled, and every few minutes would say, "You are forgiven."

# RANDOLPH

Randolph doesn't know how to fish. He likes the idea of fishing, wants to stand in a cold, swiftly-moving river in dappled sunlight and catch something, or not catch something, it doesn't matter which. He drives to the strip mall and parks in the parking lot and goes into the big sporting goods store everyone in town likes or has heard of. There are too many fishing rods to choose from.

# THE NEW CRUCIFIXIONS

People recorded them on mobile devices and posted footage of them online.

# THE HOPE

It wasn't dead it

was dormant.

# THE ZOO WITHOUT CREATURES

You could walk in
and out

of cages, lie
inside them

with your eyes
closed, and sleep

or pretend to sleep.

# BOOK III

They lifted the anchors and trusted themselves to the mercy of the sea, at the same time unlashing the tiller; then they hoisted the foresail to the breeze, and held on for the shore.

*The Acts of the Apostles 27: 40*

# THE MIRRORED HALL

It was in a house owned by a man and a woman who every morning walked together through it, holding hands, and asking each other what the other wanted to eat that morning for breakfast.

# THE NAMES OF THE DEAD

In the city was a building.
In the building was an office.
In the office was a safe.
In the safe was a key.

The key was removed from the safe by the man who worked in the office and thrown out the window of the office.

It landed on the ground at the feet of a woman who'd been walking toward the building in which the office was located.

The woman picked up the key, looked at it curiously, then shrugged, dropped it in her handbag, and entered the building with an optimistic step.

Meanwhile, the man who'd thrown the key from the office window had climbed out onto the windowsill and was preparing to jump.

He jumped.

Several minutes later, there was a knock at the office door. "Mr. Gibbons?" a male voice said. "Mr. Gibbons? Your new secretary is here."

# THE WITCH

He lived in a building near
a park through which he walked
his dog every morning before work.

# THE BLOODLETTING

They would catch you in autumn, string you
up by your ankles to a branch
of a leafless
tree.

# DESPERADO

The outlines of three horsemen who'd appeared on the opposite ridge at sundown would otherwise have struck him as beautiful.

# THE FAMINE

Someone was tolling

bells far away, and someone

nearby was tolling

bells too.

# THE ENVY

It came through
the vents, like gas.

# THE MEN ON THE BEACH

They stood alone or in groups, saying
nothing, their arms

at their sides, their eyes open, the tide
coming in and going

out.

# THE WORKAHOLIC

In the woods behind the cemetery in which he had been buried, one squirrel chased another squirrel down the trunk of a tree.

# THE SADNESS OF TREES

Two men and two
women quickly

walked past two
men and two

women who were slowly
walking past two men and two

women who
were standing.

# THE AVALANCHE

White on white
on white on
white on white.

# MIKE, THIRTEEN

Mike, thirteen, steals a can of Coke from the cooler in back of the old store. That night, he dreams he is caught, but the next morning he can't remember his dreams. It is summer. The can of Coke is at his friend's house, on the ping pong table. He didn't leave it there on purpose. He wasn't thirsty when he stole it.

Mike turns fourteen. His friend is already fourteen, and there are other things to do. The can of Coke has been drunk a long time ago, by someone in the family of Mike's friend. The can has been crushed and recycled. The old store still is there.

The old store is gone when Mike returns from college. A new store is there. The new store sells much the same merchandise as the old store, but with a little friendlier service.

Mike's friend gets married. Mike died in a motorcycle accident two years before. The motorcycle accident was ridiculous in that it didn't occur on a highway, or even on a road, but in the driveway of a house in a different state. When Mike's friend heard about the accident, he'd asked how it had happened, and was told in a voice of quiet, self-indulgent incredulity. At the wedding, and then again at the reception, he remembers asking the question, and the way in which the question was answered.

# THE OFFSPRING

Laughter and teeth, laughter
and teeth, laughter and teeth.
Laughter.

# THE PARANOID CAT

It was alone in the house when it thought it heard something. It sat very still for a long time, its head turned in the direction from which it thought it had heard the sound come. Finally it turned back to the window out of which it had been looking, and resumed looking.

# THE STAIRS THAT WENT NOWHERE

They didn't exist until the first
person who

saw them saw them.

# THE ECSTATIC VISION

For months she'd been walking in one direction, subsisting at first on bread and water, and then, after she'd run out of bread, only on water, when one morning she stopped, eyes wide, and knelt.

# THE ASSASSIN

A man rode into town on horseback, and dismounted.
Then another man rode into town on horseback, and dismounted.
They made their way into the tavern, one after the other.
The first one didn't know the second one was following him.

# THE DEFENESTRATION

They dragged him, thrashing and screaming in his white nightshirt, up the stairs of his own house and into a room that had a piano in it and a nice carpet and several pieces of furniture that were not meant to be used but to be appreciated.

# THE ABSENCE OF FRIENDS

The table had been set.
The candles had been lit.

The man had seated
himself at the table.

# THE HOUSE IN THE COUNTRY

When you left the highway, you traveled down a gravel road, raising clouds of dust behind you, until you arrived at a gate that had to be opened and closed by you, or by one of the party with whom you were traveling, before you could continue beyond the gate; that is, once the gate had been opened, and you'd gone through, the gate had to be closed again before you could go any further.

# THE HOUSE FULL OF HUMAN HAIR

If you stood in the garden, and looked up at the windows on the second floor, you could see it pressed up against the windowpanes.

# THE MACHINE GUN SONG

# THE PARADE OF RABBITS

No one saw

it. It

happened after everyone
had died.

# THE MAN FOUND GUILTY OF CONTEMPT

When he was a boy, his mother had predicted this. She had wagged her finger at him, and had said, "One day they're going to find you guilty of contempt," but in her heart she had been proud.

# THE GOOD PAGAN

Where there are woods,
let there be more woods,
and where there are oceans,
let there be oceans.

# THE KILLERS

It was night. But it was closer now to morning than it was to the evening that had preceded it. People who'd been sleeping still were sleeping, and people who hadn't at first fallen asleep, either because they were unable to or because they hadn't wanted to, now were sleeping too. A weird silence pervaded the neighborhood. That is, although the normal sounds of the city could've been heard had someone been listening, beyond them was an absence of sound, a thing that could only be articulated, or felt, when its opposite was negated. Onto the street turned a vehicle that didn't have its headlights on. It was large and sleek, an automobile that didn't belong to this era, or even to the preceding era, but perhaps to the era before that. It moved slowly, not making any sound, as if its driver or its occupants were unsure what they were looking for. The moon disappeared behind a cloud.

# HONEYMOON

He found a transistor radio washed up on the beach and showed it to her, because she was interested in those things; not transistor radios in general, but items that were thrown away or lost. "See if it works," she said. He already knew it didn't work, because he'd tried it when he'd found it, before he'd shown it to her, but he tried it again anyway, knowing that when it still didn't work she'd at least have witnessed him doing what she'd thought he needed to do.

# THE MAN WHO REFRAINED FROM SPEAKING

First, his wife was curious.
Then she was annoyed.
Then she was angry.
Then she was dismayed.

Then she sat for a long time at the windowsill, not speaking either.

The days went by.

# THE JOY THAT WAS MISTAKEN FOR SORROW

A photograph of a crying

woman had been lost and then found

and then lost again.

# THE BATTLE THAT WAS LOST BEFORE IT WAS BEGUN

As the sun rose, the men
who'd lain themselves down got
up, or got ready to get up, or got
ready to get ready to get up.

# THE TIN DRUM

Please God, let
there be a God.

# THE SNOW

A woman stood at her kitchen window one morning wearing a bathrobe and drinking coffee from a mug while her husband stood behind her, also wearing a bathrobe but not yet drinking coffee because he had woken a few minutes after she had woken and had only now appeared in the kitchen, after she had.

# THE HOLY WATER

A man who was boiled
in it came to no
harm.

# THE SKY BENEATH THE SKY

A man with no
eyes and a woman
with no eyes had a child whose eyes

served as their own.

# SINGLE

The dentist removed his plastic gloves with a snap, and said to Renee, "Well, I've got good news and bad news, which do you want first?"

"The bad news," said Renee decisively. "No, the good news, the good news."

The dentist laughed. He was in his thirties, about the same age as Renee, but married.

# THE BOOK THAT WOULDN'T BURN

Writing that appeared on its pages when it was closed disappeared when it was opened.

# THE ANNULMENT

The grandson wanted the grandmother to tell him a story while his mother, the grandmother's daughter, was out. "I'll tell you a story," said the grandmother, "but only if you tell me one first. What kind of day did you have today at school?" The grandson, who was in one of the lower grades in elementary school, thought for a moment, and then said, "A good one, I guess. We painted eggs that Mrs. Crusoe brought in." "And what color did you paint them?" asked the grandmother. "Red," said the boy. "I'll wager you didn't," said the grandmother. She was knitting while she spoke, and the boy watched the needles as she moved them in what seemed to him a complex and confusing way. "What's wager?" said the boy. "Is it like a bet of some kind?" The grandmother told him yes, it was, but that she was only joking, that of course she believed he had painted the eggs red.

# THE WINDING SHEET

It smelled
like myrrh.

# THE WOMEN WHO SPOKE IN QUIET VOICES

One day, while they were working in a field in which cornstalks grew in equal rows, rain began to fall. The rain fell on their hair and on their shoulders and on their clothing and on their cheeks and on their foreheads and on their fingers and on the backs of their hands, but it didn't fall so hard that they were unable to continue their work. They moved steadily through the rows, removing ears of corn from the husks, and dropping what they'd removed into large linen bags they'd slung over their shoulders.

# THE RIVER

It froze.
It thawed.

A bird and then another bird

flew by.

# THE DRUMS OF HEAVEN

A man who for years had been mourning the death of his wife by not coming out of the bedroom he and his wife had shared, and in which his wife had died, died.

# THE GOOD THIEF

No, no, yes.
No, no, yes.
No, no, no.

# FORTY-THREE

A woman died in our apartment before it was our apartment. I always imagined her as an old woman because we were told she had died in her sleep.

# THE WOMAN WHO LIVED
# IN THE DESERT

A man who was going to paint her portrait drove out from the city along a highway that wasn't often used, his canvas and paintbrushes and paints in the trunk of his car. The day was sunny. He had the windows rolled down. He spent the time driving thinking what colors he would use to paint her hair.

# THE NARROW ROAD TO THE INTERIOR

Moonlight. The sound
of hooves rapidly
approaching. And then
the horse itself, visible
to us who are hiding
from it in the underbrush.

# THE OTHER LAURA

There were two Lauras in our second grade class. One of them I had a crush on, but so did most of the boys, and maybe even some of the girls. Exuberance and looks are what she had, and might still have. Running and laughing were what she liked doing and was good at. The other Laura never talked. She talked, but with tiny movements of her tiny mouth, almost as if she wasn't there. Volume, we called her. As in volume, we need volume! The other Laura we simply called Laura.

# DEAD

The house at the end of the street has no front door, though in every other way it is like a normal house, or, anyway, like the other houses on this street. It has a lawn that has recently been mowed, it has a mailbox at the end of its walk, it has a driveway and a garage, it seems to just sit there in the sun. I wander around it, looking up at the windows, finding in the backyard an old man sitting in a lawn chair, asleep, though beside him on the grass is a tiny portable radio, which is off. I wake him by touching his shoulder, which is bare, and when he squints up at me, shielding his eyes with a large wrinkled hand, I flash him my badge, identifying myself as a member of the government agency to which I belong. "Oh, you again," he says, because I have visited him here before. "I thought I already explained this to you. I don't know what happened to the door. One day it was there and the next day it wasn't. Just filled in with wall. Now I simply go in and out through the windows. Is that such a crime?" He looks around, and when he doesn't see my partner, he says, "Where was that pretty girl who was here with you last time, I liked her better than you."

# THE TWO HORSES

The first one died.
The second one died.

# THE TRANCE

One morning, a woman who usually caught the train to work walked to the train station, as if she was going to catch the train, and then stood on the platform without moving as trains came and went every fifteen minutes for the rest of the day.

# THE WARRANT

Two men knock on the door of a house that they suspect is empty, but that they don't know for certain is empty, and that in fact is not empty.

# A WORKING LUNCH

The actor said he didn't want to play the part of Jesus. Then he changed his mind and said it wasn't that he didn't want to play the part of Jesus but that he couldn't. "It wouldn't feel right," he said. "Are you religious?" asked the director, handing him a cigarette, and lighting both it and his own. "Because let me assure you, I have my own reservations. But that isn't to say I don't think we can do it. A movie, remember, can be a work of devotional art. It's not necessarily entertainment." The actor considered this as they smoked. A waitress came and cleared away their plates. "It was great, thank you," the director said to the waitress. "Do you mind if he and I chat a little longer?"

# THE FASTEST GUN IN THE WEST

Into the saloon one night, three men came looking for him, and found him playing cards at a table with three other men, two of whom were drunk, and one of whom was almost drunk.

# THE THREE SPIES

The first spy was caught. The authorities put him in an interrogation room and interrogated him. But he said nothing. So he was summarily killed. Then the second spy was caught. The authorities put him in an interrogation room and interrogated him. But he too said nothing. So he was summarily killed. Finally, the third spy was caught. The authorities said to him, "We have already found your two colleagues. They are no longer at large. What need have we to seek information from you?"

# THE MAN WHO COLLECTED TEETH

He lived in an apartment in a part of town that was close to the rail yards and that always seemed to be cold and wet.

# THE LOVER

After the casket containing the woman's body had been lowered into the ground, and after the mourners had departed, and after the soil that had been mounded nearby had been deposited in the grave by the two quiet men who worked in the cemetery, and after those men themselves had disappeared, a man who had not been among the mourners arrived, and stood where the mourners had been standing.

# THE HUNTER AND THE HOUND

On the first day of snow that year, the hunter left the cabin with his hound, and together they started through the woods in the direction of the clearing where the hunter's mother and sister still lived, in a cabin like his own. On the way, the hunter got lost, and he stopped beneath a tree whose trunk was so wide that he couldn't have encircled it with his arms had the notion to do so occurred to him. Above him, the wind rustled the branches, which reached so high he couldn't see where they ended and the sky began. A few cold snowflakes landed on his cheeks. "Well," he said to the hound, who cocked its head and wagged its tail whenever the hunter spoke. "We have two choices. Actually three. We can return to the cabin, or stay here under this tree, or keep trying to find the clearing. I thought I remembered where it was, but it's been so long since I visited. What do you want to do?" The hound, of course, said nothing, and because the hunter could not decide on his own, he removed a harmonica from inside his heavy, old coat, and started playing. He played for exactly fifteen minutes, at which point he returned the harmonica to his coat, and looked expectantly in the direction into which he was facing. A moment later his sister appeared, wearing a coat like his and boots with a thick, wool lining. "Hello," he said. "I lost my way. Do you remember Viggo?" His sister smiled at the hound, at which point the hound went up to her, wagging its tail.

# THE APOSTLE

He wore a dark suit that was a little tattered, and a white shirt that was missing a button, and a navy blue tie that he'd learned how to tie from a book he'd found in a bookstore owned by a woman who wondered where he was headed and who said she liked his beard.

# THE TREE AND THE SKY

"We are the last two men alive," said one bearded man to another. "Whoever dies first will be buried by the one who himself will never be buried."

# NEW YEAR

Reggie was the only black kid in our third grade class. I told my mother I wanted to be friends with him. My mother said I should try to be friends with everyone.

# THE SEA OF GALILEE

At night, a man
walks and then
runs and then walks

along the shore.

# ACKNOWLEDGEMENTS

"The Empty Airport," "The Three Dogs," "The Flogging," "The Woman Without a Face" and "The Ghosts of Men Who Died Without Confessing Their Sins" appeared in *The Adirondack Review;*

"The Children Who Ran Rampant" and "Dead" appeared in *elimae;*

"The Man Who Beat His Dog" and "Desperado" appeared in *Corium;*

"Curtains" appeared in *Johnny America;*

"Reunion" appeared in *Alaska Quarterly Review;*

"The Churches That Burned," "The Disappearance of Shopping Malls," "The Men Who Jumped to Their Deaths" and "The Famine" appeared in *Stoked;*

"The Ammunition," "The Doppelgängers" and "The Sitcom" appeared in *Barrelhouse;*

"Only Wall," "The Man Who Collected Teeth" and "The House Full of Human Hair" appeared in *The Cortland Review;*

"The Parade of Rabbits" and "The Apostle" appeared in *Carolina Quarterly;*

"The Drums of Heaven," "The Stairs That Went Nowhere," "The Tree and the Sky," "The Trance" and "The Man Found Guilty of Contempt" appeared in *Gesture;*

"The Enormous Spiders," "The Father Who Drove His Family Over a Cliff," "The Assassin" and "The Return of the Guillotine" appeared in *New Delta Review;*

"A Comedy for the Old West," "Honeymoon" and "A Working Lunch" appeared in *Wigleaf;*

"New Year" and "Say No" appeared in *Hobart,* online;

"The Other Laura" and "Forty-three" appeared in *Beeswax;*

"The Information" and "Contagion" appeared in *Short FICTION;*

"A Minnesota Divorce" and "Sims" appeared in *Keyhole Digest;*

"Seconds" appeared in *Barn Owl Review;*

"A Rugged Coast" and "Single" appeared in *Word Riot;*

"Mike, Thirteen" appeared in *Green Mountains Review;*

"The Forgotten Story" and "The Man with the Straight Blade" appeared in *Small Doggies;*

"The Insane Laughter," "The Swarm of Mosquitoes," "The Sadness of Trees" and "The House That Fell Into the Sea" appeared in *Death Hums*.

The title of this book is taken from a book by the American Trappist monk Thomas Merton (1915-1968).

## If I Falter at the Gallows

### Edward Mullany

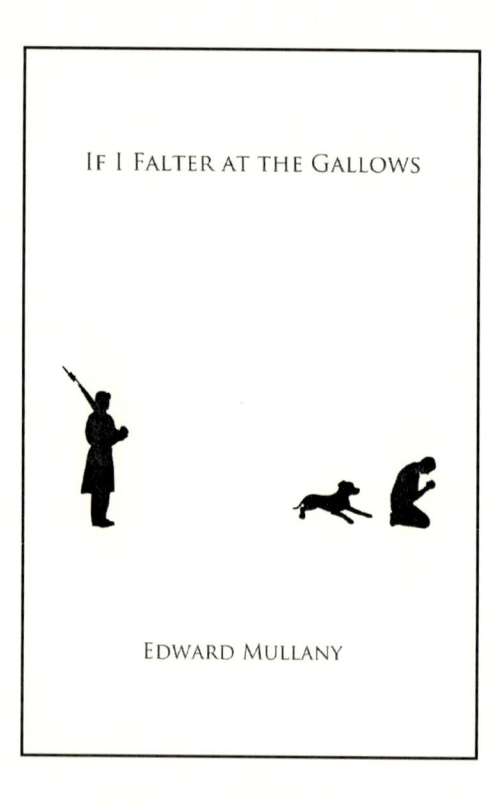

Also read Edward Mullany's first book, *If I Falter at the Gallows*, available at PublishingGenius.com and better bookstores.

| | |

The poems of Edward Mullany are both seeing things and "seeing things." They are devices that help us help ourselves to all the mirages and illusions—and then some—that we know to be true. – Graham Foust, author of *A Mouth in California*

| | |

One of my favorite things about Publishing Genius is how often their books force me to reimagine and rearrange my ideas of what language can and should be, what language can and should do. – *Vouched Books*

*find out more at www.PublishingGenius.com*